First World War
and Army of Occupation
War Diary
France, Belgium and Germany

32 DIVISION
97 Infantry Brigade
Manchester Regiment
52nd Battalion
16 March 1919 - 31 October 1919

WO95/2404/2

The Naval & Military Press Ltd
www.nmarchive.com
Published in association with The National Archives

Published by

The Naval & Military Press Ltd

Unit 10 Ridgewood Industrial Park,

Uckfield, East Sussex,

TN22 5QE England

Tel: +44 (0) 1825 749494

www.naval-military-press.com

www.nmarchive.com

This diary has been reprinted in facsimile from the original. Any imperfections are inevitably reproduced and the quality may fall short of modern type and cartographic standards.

© **Crown Copyright**
Images reproduced by permission of The National Archives, London, England, 2015.

Contents

Document type	Place/Title	Date From	Date To
Heading	WO95/2404/2		
Heading	Lancashire Division (Late 32nd Division) 97th Infy Bde (3rd Lancs Infy Bde) 52nd Bn Manchester Regt 1919 Mar 1919 Oct		
War Diary	Dunkirk	16/03/1919	16/03/1919
War Diary	Siegburg-Mulldorf	19/03/1919	19/03/1919
War Diary	Geistingen	22/03/1919	22/03/1919
War Diary	Dambroich	27/03/1919	27/03/1919
War Diary	Geistingen	30/03/1919	17/06/1919
War Diary	Dambroich	19/06/1919	19/06/1919
War Diary	Geistingen	26/06/1919	30/06/1919
Operation(al) Order(s)	52nd Bn. Manchester Regt. Operation Order No. 3		
Miscellaneous	March Table To Accompany 52nd Bn. Manchester Regt. O.O. No. 3		
Miscellaneous	52nd. Bn. Manchester-Regiment		
Miscellaneous	Programme		
War Diary	Geistingen	03/07/1919	31/07/1919
Miscellaneous	March Orders. 52nd Bn Manchester Regiment		
War Diary	Geistingen	01/08/1919	04/08/1919
War Diary	Neunkirchen	05/08/1919	30/08/1919
Miscellaneous	3rd (Manchester) Infantry Brigade.	01/09/1919	01/09/1919
Miscellaneous	Nominal Roll Of Men For Dispersal		
Operation(al) Order(s)	52nd Manchester Regiment. Order No. 1 By Lieut Colonel. G.C. Kelly D.S.O.		
Miscellaneous	Administrative Instruction Issued With Order No. 1	03/08/1919	03/08/1919
War Diary	Neunkirchen	01/09/1919	01/09/1919
War Diary	Geistingen	02/09/1919	30/09/1919
Operation(al) Order(s)	52nd Battalion Manchester Regiment. Operation Order No. 1	31/08/1919	31/08/1919
Miscellaneous	March Table A To Accompany Operation Order No 1		
Miscellaneous	March Table "B" To Accompany Operation Order No 1		
Miscellaneous	Administrative Instructions Issued In Conjunction With 52 Battalion Manchester Regiment No. 1 Dated 31.3.19	31/03/1919	31/03/1919
War Diary	Geistingen	02/10/1919	31/10/1919

WO 95/24041

LANCASHIRE DIVISION
(LATE 32ND DIVISION)
97TH INFY BDE (3RD LANCS INFY BDE)

52ND BN MANCHESTER REGT
~~MAR 1919 - JAN 1920~~
1919 MAR - 1919 OCT

52nd Manchester Regt
LCS

Army Form C. 2118.

WAR DIARY
or
INTELLIGENCE SUMMARY.
(Erase heading not required.)

Instructions regarding War Diaries and Intelligence Summaries are contained in F. S. Regs., Part II. and the Staff Manual respectively. Title pages will be prepared in manuscript.

Place	Date	Hour	Summary of Events and Information	Remarks and references to Appendices
DUNKIRK.	16.3.19	1900hrs	Battalion arrived here from GT YARMOUTH, NORFOLK, ENGLAND via DOVER.	
SIEGBURG-MÜLLDORF.	19.3.19	1200hrs	Departed from DUNKIRK by train 1450hrs 17.3.19 via BAILLEUL, ARMENTIERES, LILLE, TOURNAI, GELLINGEN, NAMUR, CHARLEROI, HUY, LIÈGE, VERVIERES to SIEGBURG-MÜLLDORF. Two companies B + C billeted at SIEGBURG-MÜLLDORF. Two companies A + D billeted at NIEDER-PLEIS.	
GEISTINGEN	22.3.19	1900hrs	Two companies left SIEGBURG-MÜLLDORF for GEISTINGEN. Batt took over left sub sector of Outpost line from 1/5th Border Regt. B Coy placed on left at WARTH. C Coy placed on right at ROTT.	
DAMBROICH.	27.3.19	1900hrs	A + D companies left NIEDER-PLEIS. A company DAMBROICH. D company billeted at GEISTINGEN.	
GEISTINGEN	30.3.19	1200hrs	Major G. DEVLIN 2nd in Command left the Battalion to take over duties at 9th Infantry Brigade. Capt W.G. SWAIN. Succeeded him	

{signature}
Lieut. Colonel,
Commanding, 52nd (Grad.) Bn. Manchester Regt.

Army Form C. 2118.

WAR DIARY
or
INTELLIGENCE SUMMARY
(Erase heading not required.)

Instructions regarding War Diaries and Intelligence Summaries are contained in F. S. Regs, Part II. and the Staff Manual respectively. Title Pages will be prepared in manuscript.

Place	Date	Hour	Summary of Events and Information	Remarks and references to Appendices
GEISTINGEN.	2.4.19	—	G.O.C. Brigade Lieut. Colonel W. H. TRAILL, C.M.G., D.S.O., visited the Outpost line.	
GEISTINGEN.	21.4.19.	—	General Sir W. R. ROBERTSON, G.C.B., K.C.V.O., D.S.O., A.D.C. visited the Outpost line.	Map Reference Siegburg 3056
GEISTINGEN.	25.4.19.	—	Lieut. Colonel G. C. KELLY, D.S.O. resumed Command of the Battalion vice Lieut. Colonel C. WAN LISS. During the whole of the month B & C Companies were holding the Outpost Line (WARTH & ROTT) with A & D Companies in reserve at DAMBROICH and GEISTINGEN, respectively.	

(signature)
Lieut. Colonel,
Commanding 2nd (Regular) Bn. Manchester Regt.

Army Form C. 2118.

WAR DIARY
or
INTELLIGENCE SUMMARY.
(Erase heading not required.)

Instructions regarding War Diaries and Intelligence Summaries are contained in F. S. Regs., Part II. and the Staff Manual respectively. Title pages will be prepared in manuscript.

Place	Date	Hour	Summary of Events and Information	Remarks and references to Appendices
GEISTINGEN	2.5.19		"A" Coy moved from DAMBROICH to relieve "B" Coy at WRATH of Outpost duties. "B" Coy moved to DAMBROICH	
GEISTINGEN	3.5.19		"C" Coy moved to GEISTINGEN from ROTT. "D" Coy moved from GEISTINGEN to ROTT to take over Outposts duties from "C" Coy.	
GEISTINGEN	9.5.19		H.R.H. The DUKE of CONNAUGHT, K.G., K.T., G.C.M.G., G.C.V.O., visited the Outpost Line & Batt. area.	
			From 3.5.19 to end of month "A" & "D" Coys held the Outpost Line (WRATH & ROTT) with "B" & "C" Coys in reserve at DAMBROICH & GEISTINGEN	

Hully
Lieut. Colonel.
Commanding 5/2nd (Brnf.) Bn. Manchester Regt.

Army Form C. 2118.

WAR DIARY 52nd Manchester
or
INTELLIGENCE SUMMARY
(Erase heading not required.)

Instructions regarding War Diaries and Intelligence Summaries are contained in F.S. Regs., Part II. and the Staff Manual respectively. Title Pages will be prepared in manuscript.

Place	Date	Hour	Summary of Events and Information	Remarks and references to Appendices
(1) GEISTINGEN	2/6/19	0900	The Divisional Commander, Major General Sir H.S. JEUDWINE, K.C.B. visits the Battalion Area to witness Platoon Exercise on GEISTINGEN Range.	MAP REFERENCE SIEGBURG 3036 1/25000. OPERATION ORDERS for (2) ATTACHED.
(2) GEISTINGEN.	17/6/19	—	J-3 day. Preparations for advance, in event of Germans failing to sign Peace Terms, commenced.	RCHH.
(3) DAMBROICH	19/6/19	—	"B" Company moved from DAMBROICH to SÖVEN in readiness for advance. Preparations complete.	RCHH.
(4) GEISTINGEN	29/6/19	—	Lieut. Col. G.C. KELLY, D.S.O. assumed temporary command of 3rd MANCHESTER Bde. in absence of Major General A. SOLLY FLOOD, commanding Lancs Div.	RCHH.
(5)	30/6/19	—	"A" Day.	RCHH.
(6) GEISTINGEN	30/6/19	—	"A" Company moved from WARTH to GEISTINGEN, being relieved of Out Post duties by "B" Coy from SÖVEN. "D" Coy moved to DAMBROICH to ROTT, being relieved of Out Post duties by "C" Coy from GEISTINGEN.	RCHH.

W. Palmer
MAJOR,
Lieut. Colonel,
Commanding, 52nd Bn. Manchester Regt.

SECRET.   Copy No. 15
                                                 Date. 19.8.19.

52ND. BN. MANCHESTER REGT. OPERATION ORDER NO.3.

Reference Maps. Sheet 2b, 1/100,000.
                 Siegburg, 1/25,000.

1. On "J" day the Lancashire Division will move in support to the Eastern Division along the following roads:-

    1st Brigade Group.   HENNEF - SIEGEN.

    3rd Brigade Group &)   HENNEF - WALDBROL.
    Div. H.Q.Group.   )

    2nd Brigade Group.   SIEGBURG - NEUSTADT.

    The object is to secure control of the railways and in doing so it will be essential to ensure not only as much railway stock as possible shall be captured, but that the German Railway personnel shall be prevented from leaving their posts. Although most of this work will devolve on the Eastern Division, troops of the Lancashire Division may have to assist.

2. The 52nd Bn. Manchester Regt. will move in accordance with attached March table on "J" day.

3. The 52nd Bn. Manchester Regt. plus -
    1 Section.   R.E.
    1 Section.   T.M.B.
    1 Section.   M.G.Batt.
will find the Advance Guard on "J" day.

4. Order of March :-
    "A" Coy.   )
    1 Section. R.E.   ) Finding Van Guard.

    Batt. H.Q.
    "B" Coy.
    "D" Coy.
    "C" Coy.   ) Find
    Transport of 52nd ~~Manchester Regt.~~) Main Guard.
    1 Section, M.G.Batt.
    1 Section, L.T.M.B.
    Transport of 52nd Bn Manchester Regt.

5. All troops in the Brigade Group will march in 3's. The distances to be observed in march will be those laid down under type "B" (see note on March Discipline issued by G.H.Q.)

6. Billetting party consisting of 1 N.C.O. per Coy. under Lieut. Hadfield will report at Batt.H.Q., Geistingen at A hour minus 1 hour. Billetting party will be mounted on bicycles.

7. Transport.
    Echelon A will move with Battalion. Echelon A will be as under.-
        4 Lewis Gun limbers. (one with each Coy).
        3 S.A.A.   "
        1 Bomb.   "
        1 Maltese Cart.
        4 Cookers.
        2 Water Carts.
        1 Tool limber.
        1 M.G. limber.
        3 Pack animals.

(1)   (P.T.O.)

(2)

7. **Transport. (Continued)**

Echelon B will march as per March Table under orders of Brigade Transport Officer.

8. The two lorries carrying packs and stores in charge of Lieut. Mott, and party of men detailed by Medical Officer will rendezvous at a time and place to be notified later and will move in Brigade Column in charge of an officer detailed by Bde.H.Q.

9. On "J" day the men will carry the unexpired portion of the day's ration plus one iron ration.

10. Watches will be synchronized at Batt.H.Q. at 12.00 hours daily, commencing on J-1 day. A representative from each Company will attend. The Orderly Officer will attend daily at Brigade H.Q. at 13.30 hours, commencing on J-1 day to synchronize.

11. On completion of a day's march 2 cyclist orderlies, to be detailed by O.C.Signals, will report at Brigade H.Q. One will remain at Brigade H.Q. and the other return with one of the 2 cyclist orderlies detailed the previous day.
Companies and Transport Section will report time "all in Billets" and the number of men who have fallen out.

12. The location of Battalion H.Q. after march on "J" day will be notified later.

13. "J" day and A hour will be notified later.

14. Acknowledge.

                        Whitehead Captain,
             Adjutant, 52nd Bn. Manchester Regt.

Issued at 16.00 hours through Signals.

Distribution:-

1. For A.	10. H.Q. Coy.
2.	11. O.C. Signals.
3. O.C.	12. Transport Officer.
4. 2nd-in-Command.	13. Quartermaster.
5. Adjutant.	14. Medical Officer.
6. "A" Coy.	15. Assistant Adjutant.
7. "B" Coy.	16. R.S.M.
8. "C" Coy.	17. Intelligence Officer.
9. "D" Coy.	18. 3rd Manchester Inf.Bde.
	19. File.

(2) 20. 3 Man Bde. L.M.B.
(3) 21. OC Section 206 Field Coy. R.E.
(19) 22. A Coy. 32nd Bn. M.G.C.

MARCH TABLE to accompany 52nd Bn. Manchester Regt. O.O. No.3.

Ser ial	Unit.	From.	To	Starting Point.	Time.	Route.	Remarks.
1.	1 Platoon, "A" Coy. 52nd Bn. Manchester Regt.	Warth.	WINTERSCHEID AREA.	Junction of HENNEF-EITORF and HENNEF-BROL Roads. 200 yds. N.W. of E. of WARTH. (Ref. sheet Siegburg 1/25,000)	A hour minus 9.	-	
2.	"D" Coy. 52nd Bn. Manchester Regt. less 1 pltn.	Warth.		-do-	A hour minus 6.		
3.	1 Section, 206 Field Coy. R.E.	Geistingen.		-do-	A hour minus 5.	Geistingen-Warth Road. South of railway.	
4.	"B" Coy. 52nd Bn. Manchester Regt.	Soven.		Junction of ARNH-HENNEF and WARTH-BROL roads. (Ref. sheet Siegburg, 1/25,000)	A hour minus 1.	Soven-Nippenhahn-Warth.	
5.	"D" Coy. 52nd Bn. Manchester Regt.	Rott.		-do-	A hour.	Rott-Soven-Nippenhahn-Warth.	
6.	Batt. H.Q. 52nd Bn. Manchester Regt.	Geistingen.		-do-	A hour minus 2.	Geistingen-Warth Road, South of railway.	
7.	"C" Coy. 52nd Bn. Manchester Regt.	-do-		-do-	A hour plus 1.	-do-	
8.	1 Section, M.G. Coy.	-do-		-do-	A hour plus 2.	-do-	
9.	1 Section, L.T.M. Battry.	-do-		-do-	A hour plus 3.	-do-	
10.	A Echelon, Transport, 52nd Bn. Manchester Regt.			-do-	A hour plus 4.	-do-	
11.	B Echelon, Transport, 52nd Bn. Manchester Regt.			To join Brigade Column at Geistingen under arrangements to be made between Transport Officer and Bde. Transport Officer.			

Captain,
Adjutant, 52nd Bn. Manchester Regt.

52nd. Bn. Manchester-Regiment.

PROGRAMME
OF SPORTS MEETING
held at
GEISTINGEN.

5th. July 1919.

Commencing 1400 hours.

A. Stross, Hennef-Sieg.

Event (16) ———— Tug of War (Final).

Winners ————

Event (17)   Sgt. Waywell

"A"	"B"	"C"	"D"
L/Cpl. Booth		2/Lt. Hunt	L/Cpl. Trengnove
Pte. Cole		Pte. Calvey	Sgt. Blowers
Pte. Miller		L/Cpl. Vose	L/Cpl. Foster
		L/Cpl. Reeves	L/Cpl. Heap
		Pte. Robinson	Pte. Walmsley
		Pte. Short	L/Cpl. Uren
		Pte. Kerr	Pte. Hoyle
		Pte. Armstrong	Pte. Jackson
		Pte. Brown	Pte. Smith
		Pte. Cox	Pte. Simpson

1st. ———— 2nd. ———— 3rd. ————

Event (18) ———— Hurdle Race (Final).

1st. ———— 2nd. ———— 3rd. ————

Event (19) ———— Warrant Officers' & Sergeants' Race.

1st. ———— 2nd. ———— 3rd. ————

Event (20) ———— Relay Race. (Teams of 4).

"A"	"B"	"C"	"D"
L/Cpl. Turner	Cpl. Parry	2/Lt. Smith	Cpl. Schofield
L/Cpl. Rees	Cpl. Tyler	C. S. M. Ryan	L/Cpl. Trengrove
Pte. Bryant	L/Cpl. Vaughan	Sgt. Sutcliffe	Pte. Walmsley
Pte. Almond	L/Cpl. Harrison	Sgt. Coulter	Pte. Atkinson

1st. ———— 2nd. ————

Event (21) ———— Officers' Race.

1st. ———— 2nd. ———— 3rd. ————

===== FINIS. =====

PROGRAMME.

Event (1) —————— Semi-final 100 Yards.

Heat 1.

L/Cpl. Turner	"A"	L/Cpl. Trengnove	"D"
Pte. Aird	"A"	Cpl. Schofield	"D"
Cpl. Parry	"A"	Pte. Kelly	"A"
Cpl. Tyler	"A"	L/Cpl. Vaughan	"B"
C. S. M. Ryan	"C"	Sgt. Coulter	"C"
Pte. Radford	"D"	Sgt. Sutcliffe	"C"

1st.————————— 2nd.—————————

Event (2) —————— Long Jump.

"A"	"B"	"C"	"D"
L/Cpl. Booth	Sgt. Waywell	Pte. Armstrong	Pte. Denton
Pte. Leather		L/Cpl. Reeves	Pte. Overton

1st.————————— 2nd.————————— 3rd.—————————

Event (3) —————— 220 Yards.

"A"	"B"	"C"	"D"
L/Cpl. Turner	Sgt. Miller	Sgt. Coulter	Pte. Walmsley
Pte. Bryant	Cpl. Parry	Sgt. Sutcliffe	Pte. Atkinson
Pte. Almond	Cpl. Tyler		

1st.————————— 2nd.————————— 3rd.—————————

Event (4) —————— Pillow Fighting on Poles.

"A"	"B"	"C"	"D"
Pte. Corkish	L/Cpl. Skyner	Sgt. Hurst	Pte. Walmsley
Pte. Kelly	Pte. Peel	Pte. Simpson	Pte. Jakson

1st.————————— 2nd.—————————

Event (5) —————— Final 100 Yards.

1st.————————— 2nd.————————— 3rd.—————————

Event (6) —————— High Jump.

"A"	"B"	"C"	"D"
L/Cpl. Booth	Cpl. Beaton	L/Cpl. Reeves	Pte. Walmesley
Pte. Gooder		Pte. Walley	Pte. Denton

1st.————————— 2nd.————————— 3rd.—————————

Event (7) —————— Sack Race.

"A"	"B"	"C"	"D"
Pte. Smith	L/Cpl. Skyner	L/Cpl. Calvey	Pte. Walmesley
Pte. Gill	L/Cpl. Ousby	Pte. Bonney	Pte. Bradshaw
Pte. Burns	Pte. Peel	Pte. Short	Pte. Horton

1st.————————— 2nd.————————— 3rd.—————————

Event (8) —————— 440 Yards.

"A"	"B"	"C"	"D"
L/Cpl. Rees	Sgt. Miller	2/Lt. Hunt	Pte. Radford
L/Cpl. Booth	Cpl. Vaughan	L/Cpl. Reeves	Pte. Atkinson
Pte. Phillips	Cpl. Johnson		

1st.————————— 2nd.————————— 3rd.—————————

Event (9) —————— Tug of War

"A" versus "C" — "B" versus "D"

1st.————————— 2nd.—————————

Event (10) —————— 880 Yards.

"A"	"B"	"C"	"D"
Pte. Leather	L/Cpl. Harrison	2/Lt. Smith	L/Cpl. Uren
Cpl. Stirrup	Sgt. Miller	Pte. Spencer	L/Cpl. Trengnove
Pte. Bryant		Pte. Bonny	Pte. Riley

1st.————————— 2nd.————————— 3rd.—————————

Event (11) —————— Boat Race.

1st.————————— 2nd.—————————

Event (13) —————— Hurdle.

Heat 1. **Heat 2.**

"A"	"B"	"C"	"D"
Pte. Goader		L/Cpl. Booth	"A"
Sgt. Waywell		Pte. Shepherd	"B"
Pte. Walley		L/Cpl. Marsden	"C"
Pte. Atkinson			"D"

1st.————————— 2nd.—————————

Event (14) —————— Pick-a-Back Wrestling.

"A"	"B"	"C"	"D"
Sgt. Cooper }	Cpl. Beaton }	Pte. Alexander }	Pte. Foxton }
Pte. Little }	Sgt. Waywell }	Pte. Pickup }	Pte. Madgin }
Pte. Ashton }		Pte. Wright }	Pte. Grimshaw }
Pte. Bridgehouse }		Pte. Short }	Pte. Robinson }

1st. Pair————————— 2nd. Pair—————————

Event (15) —————— One Mile.

"A"	"B"	"C"	"D"
L/Cpl. Rees	Sgt. Miller	2 Lt. Smith	L/Cpl. Uren
Pte. Milne	Cpl. Johnson	2/Lt. Hunt	Pte. Atkinson
Pte. Corkish	L/Cpl. Wrigth	C. S. M. Ryan	Pte. Smith
Pte. Hayes		Pte. Bonney	Pte. Hindle

1st.————————— 2nd.————————— 3rd.—————————

WAR DIARY or INTELLIGENCE SUMMARY

Army Form C. 2118.

of THE 52nd BATTALION, THE MANCHESTER REGT.

for JULY, 1919.

Place	Date	Hour	Summary of Events and Information	Remarks and references to Appendices
GEISTINGEN (1)	3.7.19	0800	Platoons (one each of A.B.C.D Coys) fractise Field Firing exercise on Geistingen Ranges for their part in "Platoon Efficiency Cup".	RWW
" (2)	4.7.19	0800	Platoon Efficiency but Contest in Field Firing on Geistingen Ranges, commenced by "A" Coy. "B" Coy at 1000 hrs. "C" Coy at 1400 hrs. "D" Coy at 1600 hrs.	RWW
" (3)	4.7.19	0900	Capt. W.G. SWAIN proceeded to ENGLAND for demobilisation.	RWW
" (4)	5.7.19	1400	BATTALION SPORTS. Company Cup won by "C" Coy (Programme attached)	RWW
" (5)	6.7.19	1500	Capt. E. MYATT, M.C. and 4 N.C.O's proceed to PARIS to take part in VICTORY MARCH.	RWW
" (6)	6.7.19	—	First party of 5 men proceeded to YPRES to visit the BATTLE FIELDS.	RWW
" (7)	6.7.19	—	Capt. W. WHITEHEAD (ADJUTANT) proceeded on leave to U.K. (7.7.19 – 21.7.19) his duties being carried out by Lieut. G.E. NOTT.	RWW
" (8)	7.7.19	—	G.O.C. in C. British Army of the Rhine, GENERAL SIR WILLIAM ROBERTSON visited the Battalion for a short period.	RWW

WAR DIARY
or
INTELLIGENCE SUMMARY

Army Form C. 2118.

OF THE 52ND BATTALION THE MANCHESTER REGT.
July 1919
Sheet 2.

Place	Date	Hour	Summary of Events and Information	Remarks and references to Appendices
GEISTINGEN (9)	8.7.19	0830	G.M.C. commenced on GEISTINGEN RANGE by "A" and "B" Companies	MMW
" (10)	9.7.19		G.M.C. continued by "A" and "B" Companies.	Raining
" (11)	"	1800	Final of Brigade Boxing Competition held in CANTEEN at GEISTINGEN between "A" and "B" Companies. "B" Coy. won by 4 fights to one. MAJOR GENERAL A. SOLLY-FLOOD, C.B.C.M.G. Reft to was present.	
" (12)	10.7.19	0830	G.M.C. continued but rain at 0900 hrs. made it impossible to fire more than one practice. Erection of canvas revet.	Retd. to
" (13)	10.7.19	0900	Canvas bank for one Company commenced at GEISTINGEN, by R.E.	Reserve
" (14)	11.7.19	-	Battalion Messing arrangements inspected by Camp Commandant Lancashire Division.	
" (15)	10.7.19	-	Platoon Efficiency test won by 16 Platoon "D" Company, Butler	
" (16)	11.7.19	-	Officers from various units arrive to inspect Battalion Messing arrangements	MW

WAR DIARY of the 52nd BATTALION THE MANCHESTER REGT
INTELLIGENCE SUMMARY
JULY 1919
Sheet 3

Army Form C. 2118

Place	Date	Hour	Summary of Events and Information	Remarks and references to Appendices
17) Giesthingen	15.7.19	—	G.M.C. returned by "A" Coy on GEISTINGEN RANGE, "B" Coy marking.	MHH
18) "	16.7.19	—	Major E. FAIRHURST, M.C. proceeded to U.K. on leave. Lieut. Col. G.C. KELLY DSO doing duties of Brigade + Battalion Commander	MHH MHH
19) "	18.7.19	—	Lieut. Col. G.C. KELLY returned from 3rd MANCHESTER BDE. Lieut. M.H. GILES proceeded to U.K. for demobilization of G. raining with the unit for 2 years at T.O.	RMH RMH RWhitfield
20) "	19.7.19	—	G.M.C. continued by "A" Coy on GEISTINGEN RANGE; bad weather a great hindrance.	RWhitfield
21) "	21.7.19	—	MENDEN. Platoon Competition starts at 3rd MANCHESTER BDE. SCHOOL Lt. Col. G.C. KELLY and officers proceed there to witness the performance.	RMH
22) "	22.7.19	—	Heavy rain; Competition at BDE. SCHOOL fortunes do much training	RMH

Army Form C. 2118.

WAR DIARY of the 52nd BATTALION
THE MANCHESTER REGT.
or INTELLIGENCE SUMMARY.
(Erase heading not required.)

SHEET 4   July 1919

Place	Date	Hour	Summary of Events and Information	Remarks and references to Appendices
GEISTINGEN	23.7.19	-	"D" Coy. Camp at GEISTINGEN almost complete. Rain prevented "D" Coy. moving from DAMBROICH as intended.	
"	24.7.19	-	"D" Coy. moved from DAMBROICH to canvas camp at GEISTINGEN.	Copy of Orders attached
"	25.7.19	-	Canvas camps for "A" and "HQ" coys erected in GEISTINGEN. Tents issued to "B" Coy. "C" Coy. at ROTT, "D" Coy. at Geistingen	
"	26.7.19	-	Divisional Sports held in BONN. 264 Lewis of "C" Coy. won 440 yards and 2nd. in 880 yards. Time for 440" 57 secs.	
"	27.7.19	-	Capt. W. WHITEHEAD and Lieut. J.H. MOORE proceeded to U.K. for demobilisation	
"	28.7.19	-	Platoon of 51st Manchesters inspected by BRIGADIER in Ceremonial Drill, Attack, Musketry etc. for Platoon Efficiency Cup.	
"	29.7.19	-	53 Manchester Platoon for Efficiency Cup inspected at GEISTINGEN in Drill, Platoon in Attack, &c. by MAJOR GENERAL SOLLY-FLOOD	Report
"	30.7.19	-	Inspection of No.15 Platoon under Lt. TAIT at MENDEN for Efficiency cup by MAJOR GENERAL SOLLY-FLOOD. Cup won by No.15 Platoon	Report
"	31.7.19	-	G.M.C. commenced on GEISTINGEN RANGE. B. Coy.	

J.M. [signature], Lieut. Colonel, Commanding, 52nd Bn. Manchester Regt.

Copy.   MARCH ORDERS.

"D" Company.   52nd BN Manchester Regiment.

1. The Company will march to Geistingen tomorrow and take over a tented camp.
2. Instructions for the move are as follows :-
   Reveille.   5 a.m.
   Handing in of Blankets.   6.15 a.m.
   Breakfast.   6.30 a.m.
   Cleaning up of Billets.   7.00 a.m. to 8.00 a.m.
   Inspection of Billets by Platoon
                                Commanders.   8.15 a.m.
   Company Parade.   9.00 a.m.
   DRESS. (Fighting Order).
   The Company will be divided up into 4 Parties :-
       (a). Transport Party.
       (b). Advance Party.
       (c). Main Party.
       (d). Rear Party.

(a). The transport party will consist of Company Cooker, Company Limber, and Pack Mule (Loaded).
     2 Cooks and Messing Corporal will accompany cooker.
     2 Lewis Gunners to act as escort and one man as brakesman to L.G. Limber.
     1 Groom for Pack Mule.
     The C.S.M. will detail one Sgt to take charge of the party.
     The route - BIRLINGHOVEN. NEIDER PLEIS. GEISTINGEN.
     Sgt will be responsible for correct march discipline, and that no men ride on cooker or limber, and that each man is dressed correctly all the way.
     This party will leave at 08.30 Hours dinner to be cooked en-route.

(b). Advance party will consist of O.C. Company, one N.C.O from each Platoon (Sgts), and party already at camp.
     The 4 N.C.O's will leave DAMBROICH at 9.00 a.m., and report to O.C. Company at camp. Their duties will be difined on arrival.

(c). Main party will be under command of Lieut Oliver and will consist of all ranks not included in A.B.D.
     Leave DAMBROICH at 09.30 a.m.
     Route :- OLGARTEN. GEISTINGEN.

(d). Rear party consisting of Capt Kemble :- 1 N.C.O and 6 Men.
     They will carry out all loading duties tomorrow and remain until stores are clear, proceeding to GEISTINGEN by last lorry.
     This party will retain 2 spades for filling in of refuse pit and latrines and will be responsible for leaving the Company Area clean.
     In the event of all stores not being cleared in reasonable time tomorrow they will be handed over to Chief Inhabitant.(Reuter). and receipt obtained for same.

3. GENERAL.
   (a). Sick parade tomorrow 2 p.m. Battalion aid post.
   (b). Officers kits to be sent to Company Dump by 8.00 a.m.
   (c). Officers Mess boxes will be sent to Dump by 8.30 a.m. (Prompt).
   (d). O.C. Company requires horse by 9.00 a.m. (Marching Order).
   (e). Telephone to be left where it is.
   (f). When Company gets into Camp no man will be permitted to leave it without authority is given to do so by O.C. Company.
   (g). Tents are allotted as per attached rough sketch.
   (h). Cooker will be used for all cooking until further notice.
   (i). Stable at present occupied by Company will be left clean and all manure placed in receptables for same.
   (j). Employed men and signallers will march with main party.
   (r). The Company on Guard will dismount at 8.00 a.m.

                                            H.J. RATHBONE   Capt.
                                              O.C. "D" Company.

Army Form C. 2118.

WAR DIARY of 52nd BATTALION
or
INTELLIGENCE SUMMARY. THE MANCHESTER REGT.

(Erase heading not required.)

Instructions regarding War Diaries and Intelligence Summaries are contained in F. S. Regs., Part II. and the Staff Manual respectively. Title pages will be prepared in manuscript.

Sheet 1.

Place	Date	Hour	Summary of Events and Information	Remarks and references to Appendices
1 GEISTINGEN	1.9.19	—	Battalion de-lousing commenced prior to move into tented camps GEISTINGEN	Appx A
2 "	2.9.19	—	Battalion de-lousing continued. Notice received Bn. to be ready to move at an early date.	Appx A Appx B
3 "	3.9.19	—	Battalion de-lousing completed.	Appx A Appx B
4 "	4.9.19	—	Battalion moved to NEUNKIRCHEN (B.2 Coy and H.Q.). A Coy to OBERHEISTER. B Coy to HERMERATH for outpost duty. Copy of move order attached.	Appx C Move order attached
5 NEUNKIRCHEN	5.9.19	—	Major General A. SOLLY-FLOOD C.B. C.M.G. D.S.O. inspected outpost line. Three area of Battalion	Appx D
6 "	6.9.19	—	do	Appx E
7 "	7.9.19	—	Move from GEISTINGEN completed - i.e. Stores etc. and rear parts moved to new area	Appx F
8 "	8.9.19	—	Inspection of new area by G.O.C. LANCASHIRE DIVISION. Lieut. Col. F.C. KELLY D.S.O. proceeded on leave to U.K.	Appx G
9 "	9.9.19	—	G.O.C. Lancashire Division visited the Battalion. D. Coy began their G.M.C.	Appx H
10 "	10.9.19	—	G.M.C. continued by B & D Companies.	Appx I
11 "	11.9.19	—	36 Other ranks proceeded for dispersal prior to re-enlistment in Post Hostilities Army.	Non Roll attached
12 "	12.9.19	—	B. Coy. continued G.M.C.	Appx J Appx K
13 "	13.9.19	—	Lt. Col. TRAIL a/Brigadier 3rd MANCHESTER BDE. visited Bn. area northerly coy. Lieut. Q.M. WARBURTON W.R. 1/6 MANCHESTER Regt. taken on strength of the Battalion.	Appx L
14 "	14.9.19	—	Bn. holiday in place of August 4th when Bn. moved to NEUNKIRCHEN	Appx M

WAR DIARY of 52nd BATTALION THE MANCHESTER REGIMENT
or INTELLIGENCE SUMMARY

Army Form C. 2118.

Sheet 2.

Place	Date	Hour	Summary of Events and Information	Remarks and references to Appendices
NEUNKIRCHEN	18.8.	—	Lt Col TRAILL a/Brigadier 3rd MANCHESTER BRIGADE visited Bn & witnessed field firing scheme carried out by B & D Companies on BRÜCKHAUSEN Range	Salcott
"	19.8	"	Lt Col Harvey I.O.M.G.S. G.H.Q. inspected messing & cookhouses &c. NEUNKIRCHEN area	Salcott
"	20.8	"	Lt Col Harvey I.O.M.G.S. G.H.Q. inspected messing A Coy at OBERHEISTER	Salcott
"	21.8	"	G.M.C. continued by D Coy at BRUCKHAUSEN Range	Salcott
"	22.8	"	do	Salcott
"	23.8	"	Whist drive & dance for men of Battalion stationed at NEUNKIRCHEN	Salcott
"	25.8	"	Lt Col KELLY D.S.O. returned from leave & took over command of 3rd Man Inf Bde	Salcott
"	26.8	"	Dinner followed by concert given by Sgts Mess Bn at NEUNKIRCHEN	Salcott
"	27.8	"	Lt Col KELLY D.S.O. returned to the Battalion from 3rd (Man) Brigade	Salcott
"	28.8	"	Inspection of NEUNKIRCHEN, HERMERATH, OBERHEISTER area by officers of 23rd Royal Fusiliers 3rd London Brigade	Salcott
"	29.8	"	Inspection of C Coy at HERMERATH and roads by Lt Col G.C. KELLY D.S.O. Also inspection of B and HQ Coys at NEUNKIRCHEN	Salcott
"	30.8	"	Inspection of D Coy at NEUNKIRCHEN by Lt Col G.C. KELLY D.S.O.	Salcott

MKelly
Commanding 52nd Bn. Manchester

3rd (Manchester) Infantry Brigade.

             Herewith War Diary for the month of
August.

                                    [signature]
                                    Lieut. Colonel.
                        Commanding 52nd Bn Manchester Regt.

1/9/19.
AW

Nominal Roll of Men for Dispersal:- 16/2/

36800	Sgt Brent	A.
36533	Pte Smathers	W.
36366	L/Cpl Coles	W.A.
37051	Pte Wild	E.
37042	Pte Page	G.
36798	Pte Midas	M.
36695	Pte McDonnell	A.
36730	Pte Williams	J.
36766	Pte Uber	H.
36762	Pte Trinkett	F.
36771	Pte Wright	J.
36629	Pte Davidson	E.
36651	Pte Glover	W.
36628	Pte Dalvey	M.
36633	Pte Fielding	L.
36636	Pte Allenby	A.
36627	Pte Douglas	L.
36655	Pte Daddy	P.
36460	Pte Kerrighan	D.
36146	Pte Boardman	J.
36147	Pte Bergin	J.M.
36290	L/Cpl Mason	F.
36621	Pte Bauro	J.
36556	Cpl Moran	J.
36434	Pte Morris	H.B.
36676	Pte Kerr	A.
36423	Pte Haigh	L.
36461	Pte Harper	W.R.
36383	Pte Davis	A.
37044	Pte Craig	E.
	L/Cpl Ridgway	J.
36634	Pte Doyle	W.
36602	Pte Brown	G.H.
36712	Pte Roberts	S.
36705	Pte Pollard	R.
36629	Pte Nelson	H.

This man has been recalled from leave. Will report in the morning.

(signature)
Lieut.
A/Adjutant 52nd Bn Manchester Regiment.

52ND MANCHESTER REGIMENT. ORDER NO.1.
BY LIEUT. COLONEL. G. L. KELLY D.S.O.

Reference Map. 1/2500 4S.SE.

1. The Battalion will move tomorrow to relieve the 52nd Royal Sussex Regt in the NEUNKIRCHEN Area.

2. Dispositions on completion of relief will be as follows :-
   "C" Coy.   HEIMERZAH and posts 16 to 22.
   "A" Coy.   OBERHEISTER and posts 23 to 28.
   Bn H.Q. "B" and "D" Companies NEUNKIRCHEN.

3. (1) "C" and "A" Coys will move by lorry from ROTT and GEISTINGEN respectively at 07.00 hours under Company arrangements.
   5 lorries are allotted to each of these Companies.

   (11) The remainder of the Battalion (less "B" Company) will be formed up at 13.00 hours, ready to move off, on the road immediately West of Geistingen Church.
   Order of March. Battalion H.Q. "D" Coy. Transport.
   "B" Coy will join the column immediately in rear of "D" Coy, as it passes through WARTH.

   (111) Route - ALLNER - EROL - INGERSAUEL - NEUNKIRCHEN.

   (1V) Dress - Fighting Order with caps.

   (V) Company limbers and cookers will move with the Transport.

4. The present area will be taken over as follows :-
   (a) ROTT AND NOS.1 and 2 Posts. By one Company 51st King's.
   Parties to relieve Control Posts will probably not arrive till after "C" Company has moved off.
   "C" Company will leave an Officer to hand over ROTT and the Posts and to bring the personnel of the posts to the new area.

   (b) WARTH AND NOS.3 and 4 Posts.
   By one Company 51st King's.
   "B" Company will act as in (a) above.

   (c) GEISTINGEN. Advanced Parties of 51st Manchesters will take over Geistingen and camps from the Battalion Rear Party under Lt. Oliver.
   51st Manchesters will not move into Geistingen until the 5th inst.

5. On completion of reliefs in the new area Companies will notify Battalion H.Q. at NEUNKIRCHEN accordingly.

6. Administrative instructions are being issued separately.

7. Acknowledge.

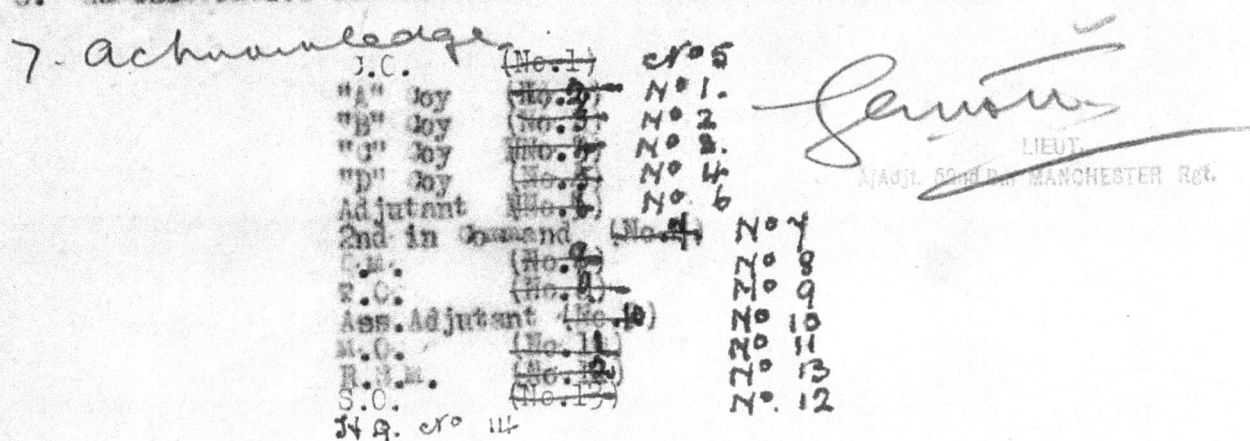

LIEUT.
A/Adjt. 52nd Bn MANCHESTER Regt.

I.C.	(No.1)	No 5
"A" Coy	(No.2)	No 1
"B" Coy	(No.3)	No 2
"C" Coy	(No.4)	No 3
"D" Coy	(No.5)	No 4
Adjutant	(No.6)	No 6
2nd in Command	(No.7)	No 7
Q.M.	(No.8)	No 8
T.O.	(No.9)	No 9
Ass.Adjutant	(No.10)	No 10
M.O.	(No.11)	No 11
R.S.M.	(No.12)	No 13
S.O.	(No.13)	No 12
J.A.		No 14

Ratcock

ADMINISTRATIVE INSTRUCTIONS ISSUED
WITH ORDER NO.1.

1. **"C" Company.**
   (a) 5 Lorries will arrive ROTT 07.00 hours 4th inst.
   (b) The Company less Control Posts and 1 Officer will then move off.
   (c) If possible all Company Stores will be taken on the lorries.
   (d) The Officer and Control Posts personnel will march to Batt.H.Q. as soon as relieved, if all Company Stores are cleared. If not, a lorry will be sent to them on return of the original five.
   (e) All tents, tent-boards, ablution benches and latrines will be handed over to 51st King's.
   (f) Maps, Order Boards etc. will be also handed over.
   (g) An inventory will be made of all stores handed over, and a receipt obtained.
   (h) Company Limber and Company Cooker will be despatched to Transport Officer as soon as possible after breakfasts. Both to be properly loaded and free from odd articles.

2. **"A" Company.**
   (a) 5 lorries will arrive Geistingen 07.00 hours 4th inst. and Coy will move off, less 1 N.C.O. and 6 men as rear party.
   (b) As many Coy Stores as possible will be taken in the lorries.
   (c) A Coy Dump will be formed at the present Coy Office.
   (d) Company Limber and Coy Cooker will join the T.O. as soon as possible after breakfasts.

3. **"D" Company.**
   (a) A Company dump will be formed and left in charge of 1 N.C.O. and 6 men.
   (b) Essentials required for the first night will be kept separate from remaining material.
   (c) Tents, boards, ablution benches and latrines will be left in situ.

4. **BN. H.Q.**
   (a) As per "D" Company

5. **"B" Company.**
   (a) As per "D" Company as regards dumps, and as per "C" Company as regards Control Posts.

6. **LORRIES.**
   (a) One lorry will report at Bn.H.Q. at 07.00 hours to take advanced parties of H.Q. "B" and "D" Coys to NEUNKIRCHEN.
   Lt.Simpson will accompany these parties.
   2nd in Command will proceed at the same hour by car. These Advanced Parties will report at Bn.H.Q. at 06.45 hours 4th inst.
   (b) The 5 lorries allotted to "C" Coy will pick up an Officer of "B" Coy. on passing through EARTH. This Officer will bring them back to Bn.H.Q. after De-bussing "C" Company.
   (c) The 5 lorries allotted to "A" Coy will be in charge of Lt.Alexander who will bring them back to Bn.H.Q. after de-bussing "A" Coy.
   (d) The 10 lorries will then be used for
       (a) Clearing Coy Dumps of Essentials.
       (b) Clearing Q.M. Stores.
   (e) Lieut. Oliver will be in charge of the rear parties Bn H.Q. "B" & "D" Coys, and will use them for loading lorries at Coy Dumps then at Q.M. Stores and both Dumps, and finally as guard over remaining stores not cleared tomorrow.
   Rear party of "A" Coy will move off with "A" Coys last lorry load.

7. **HANDING OVER.**
   Lieut.Oliver will hand over to advanced parties of 51st Manchesters all tents, boards, ablution benches, latrines etc. in the area and obtain receipts.

(CONTINUED)

8. Companies, Q.M. and T.O. will report to Lieut.Oliver as early as possible tomorrow morning situation of their Dumps and order of priority of delivery.

9. Lieut.Oliver will hand over to 51st Manchesters Advanced Parties all maps, defence schemes, etc. and all Civil Administration documents in connection with the present area.

10. Rations for the 5th inst. will be delivered by lorry to Geistingen at 10.45 a.m. and conducted to BRUCHHAUSEN by Lieut.Carle.

11. Acknowledge.

Lieut.
Adj/Adjutant 52nd Battalion Manchester Regiment.

3/8/19.
"A" Coy. (No. 1)
"B" Coy. (No. 2)
"C" Coy. (No. 3)
"D" Coy. (No. 4)
H.Q. Coy. (No. 5)
J.O. (No. 6)
Adjut. (No. 7)
2nd. in Command (No. 8)
Q.M. (No. 9)
T.O. (No. 10)
Asst. Adjt. (No. 11)
M.O. (No. 12)
S.O. (No. 13)
R.S.M. (No. 14)

Army Form C. 2118.

WAR DIARY or INTELLIGENCE SUMMARY

of the 52ⁿᵈ BN. THE MANCHESTER RGT.

(Erase heading not required.)

SHEET 1

Place	Date	Hour	Summary of Events and Information	Remarks and references to Appendices
1 Neunkirchen	1.9.19	0930	Advance parties leave NEUNKIRCHEN en route for GEISTINGEN, the advance camp.	RHH
2 GEISTINGEN	2.9.19		Battⁿ move from NEUNKIRCHEN area to GEISTINGEN area. Being relieved by 23ʳᵈ Royal Fusiliers. "B" and "H.Q." Companies moved by motor-lorries; "A" and "C" Companies marched. Being a great distance to travel, "B" Coy also moved by lorry so it was to proceed to R.T.T. to take on the ot. Post line there.	Move orders & admin instructions (motorlorries) (strides) RHH
3 GEISTINGEN	5.9.19		MAJOR E. FAIRHURST MC proceeded to Lancashire leave for duties of G.S.O. 2. Capt. J.H. RATHBONE takes on duties of 2ⁿᵈ in Command.	RHH
"	4.9.19		"C" Company commenced firing GMC on GEISTINGEN RANGE	RHH
"	9.9.19	0900	Scheme for bathing and fumigation of Battⁿ drawn up and arrangements made at Barlinghoven BIRLINGHOVEN Baths. Fumigation of clothing to be done by a "FODEN".	
		2130	Information received that "FODEN" not available. Arrangements postponed.	RHH

Army Form C. 2118.

WAR DIARY
or
INTELLIGENCE SUMMARY.
(Erase heading not required.)

Sheet 2.

Instructions regarding War Diaries and Intelligence Summaries are contained in F. S. Regs., Part II. and the Staff Manual respectively. Title pages will be prepared in manuscript.

Place	Date	Hour	Summary of Events and Information	Remarks and references to Appendices
GEISTINGEN	10.9.19	0800	Bathing and Fumigation commenced at KURHAUS, GEISTINGEN. A Coy. completed by 1600 hrs.	AWR
"	11.9.19		Capt H.J. RATHBONE proceeded to U.K. for repatriation to SOUTH AFRICA. Capt E. MYATT, returned from leave assumed duties of 2nd in Command	AWR
"	12.9.19	0900	Bathing and Fumigation commenced at BIRLINGHOVEN. "B" Coy, L.T.M.B. and a party of "HQ" Coy finished by 1500 hrs. C Coy continue firing GMG on GEISTINGEN RANGE.	Reff.
"	13.9.19	0800	Bathing continued. C Coy and part of HQ Coy finished by 1100 hrs. Bathing contests held in Bathing Pool in the Sieg HENNEF. Swimming tests held.	AWR
"	14.9.19		Major General A. SOLLY FLOOD C.B, C.M.G. visited Batt. for conference on demobilisation.	AWR
"	16.9.19	1700	Batt. Aquatic Sports held in BATHING POOL, on the SIEG, HENNEF. Some good swimming and much amusement. Unfortunately water very cold.	AWR
"	18.9.19		Batt. proceeded on RHINE TRIP. Train left HENNEF at 0745 arrived in	

WAR DIARY
or
INTELLIGENCE SUMMARY.
(Erase heading not required.)

Army Form C. 2118.

Sheet 3

Place	Date	Hour	Summary of Events and Information	Remarks and references to Appendices
13. GEISTINGEN	13.9.19		BONN at 0845. Steamer left BONN at 0930: arrived COBLENZ 1430. A delightful day.	RWW
"	14.		10 men proceeded to U.K. for demob.	RWW
"	15.		Final of Brigade Boxing competition held at GEISTINGEN. 51st MANCHESTERS defeated this unit by 1 point.	RWW
"	16.		Battalion dance held in GEISTINGEN HALL. Very successful. Brigade Sports held at HENNEF. Cut won by 51st MANCHESTERS. Unfortunately the morning was very wet; the same came RWW out at about 1500 hrs. and cheered things up.	RWW
"	17.		B & C Companies amalgamated, under the command of Capt. A. ROBERTSON.	RWW
"	18.		Boxing tournament held in GEISTINGEN HALL.	
"	19.9.19		Billeting Reconnaisance carried out in GEISTINGEN, prior to movement of all troops out of canvas camp.	

[signature]
Lieut. Colonel,
Commanding 52nd Bn. Manchester Regt.

SECRET.   COPY NO. 1

52ND BATTALION MANCHESTER REGIMENT.
OPERATION ORDER NO. 1.

Ref. map sheet 2 L 1/100.000.   31. 8. 19.

1. The Battalion and 3rd Brigade L.M.B. will be relieved in Neunkirchen Area on 2nd September 1919 by the 23rd Batt. Royal Fusiliers, and will move to the Geistingen - Rott Area on the 2nd September.1919. and will be disposed in new area as follows ....

        Battalion H.Q.)
        Transport   )
        "A" Company   )
        "B" Company   )   Geistingen.
        "C" Company   )
        3rd Bde.L.M.B.)

        "D" Company   Rott - Relieving troops of the
                                51st King's Liverpool Regt.

2. "D" Company at Rott will find one Post at Rott and one Post at Seven, and one detached Platoon at FROKWINKEL.

3. Advance Parties and Companies will move as per attached March Tables A and B.

4. Completion of reliefs and arrival in new area will be reported to Battalion H.Q.

5. Receipts for Stores handed over will be sent to Battalion H.Q. by 18.00 hours 3rd inst.

6. Administrative Instructions will be issued later.

7. Acknowledge (Units of 52nd Batt Manchester Regt. and 3rd Brigade
                                                        L.M.B. only)

                                                    G.H.L. Oliver.
                                                                         Lieut.
        Act/Adjutant 52nd Battalion Manchester Regiment.

Issued through Signals at ....

Copies to
1. War Diary.
2. "
3. I.O.
4. 2nd-in-Command.
5. "A" Company.
6. "B" "
7. "C" "
8. "D" "
9. "HQ" "
10. T.O.
11. Q.M.
12. R.S.M.
13. 3rd Bde. L.M.B.
14. O i/c Signals.
15. 3rd (Manchester) Inf. Bde.
16. 23rd Batt. Royal Fusiliers.
17. 51st King's Liverpool Regt.
18. 51st Batt. Manchester Regt.
19. File.

MARCH TABLE A TO ACCOMPANY OPERATION ORDER NO............

Serial No.	Date	Unit	From	To	Hour of move	Transport arrangements.	Remarks.
1.	1.9.19.	Advance Party D Coy.	Neunkirchen	Rott	09.00 hours.	1 Lorry will report D Coy's H.Q. 08.00 hrs.	To take baken parties of stores.
2.	1.9.19.	Advance Party A Coy.	Oberholzer	Geisting	09.30 hours.	1 Lorry will report A Coy's H.Q. 08.30 hrs.	"
3.	1.9.19.	Advance Party C Coy.	"	Hormerath	09.30 hours.	1 Lorry will report C Coy's H.Q. 08.30 hrs.	"
4.	1.9.19.	Advance Party B Coy.	"	Neunkirchen	08.30 hours.	1 Lorry will report B Coy's H.Q. 08.00 hrs.	Battn lorry to be detailed by Q.M.
5.	1.9.19.	Advance Party HQ Coy.	"	"	08.30 hours.	1 Lorry will report HQ Coy's HQ 08.00 hrs.	ditto
6.	1.9.19	Advance Party 3rd Bde L.M.B.	"	"	11.30 hours.	1 Lorry will report 3rd Bde L.M.B. 11.00 hrs.	Lorry Serial No.5 to be used on second journey.

NOTES:

1. Lorries Serial Nos. 1. 2. 3. will return to NEUNKIRCHEN and report to Q.M. immediately. moves Serial Nos. 1. 2. 3. are complete. To be used by Q.M. for move of stores. These lorries will remain night 1st/and 2nd September at Neunkirchen.

2. Lorry Serial No.4 will be the Ration Lorry.

3. Advance Parties will consist of 1 Officer and 12 Other ranks, the Q.M. to arrange rations for 2nd September. Accommodation for night 1st/and 2nd September will be found in camps vacated by 51st Manchester Regt.

4. Guides from Neunkirchen to Outpost Companies for Serial Nos. 2 and 3 to be detailed by O.C. "HQ" Company.

MARCH TABLE "3" TO ACCOMPANY OPERATION ORDER NO..../....

Serial No:	Date	Unit	From	To	Hours of move.	Transport arrangements	Remarks
1.	2.9.19.	A Coy less advcd party.	Oberholster	Geistingen	On completion of relief.	5 lorries will report Coy's H.Q. 10.00 hours.	"A" Lorries report Battln H.Q. 08.00 hours.
2.	2.9.19.	C Coy less Advcd party.	Hermerath.	"	ditto	5 lorries will report Coy's H.Q. 10.00 hours.	"C" ditto
3.	2.9.19.	D Coy less advcd party.	Neunkirchen	Rott	08.00 hrs.	5 lorries will report Coy's H.Q. 07.00 hours.	"D" Lorries Serial No.1.2.3. March Table A and 2 lorries reporting 18.00 hrs 1.9.19 to be used.
4.	2.9.19.	Batt.H.Q. & Transport less advcd party. B Coy.less advce party and Rear Pty 3rd Bde LMB less advce party.	Neunkirchen	Geistingen	10.00 hrs.	Order of March. Batt. H.Q. "B" Coy 3rd Bde L.M.B. Transport.	Starting Point. Road Junction - Hospital Neunkirchen.
5.	2.9.19.	Rear Party of 1 Officer & 6 men :B Coy:-	Neunkirchen	Geistingen	On completion of duty.	Lorries Serial No.3 on second journey.	To clear all Stores and personnel from Neunkirchen.

NOTES.
1. Lorries Serial No.3 will return to Neunkirchen, and report to Q.M. immediately move Serial No.5 is complete.
2. Guides from Neunkirchen to Outpost Companies for lorry convoys Serial Nos.1 & 2 to be detailed by O.C. HQ Coy.
3. Dress for Serial No.4 will be Fighting Order with S.D.Caps, S.B. Respirators slung. Steel Helmets fastened on packs, which will be carried in M.T.

ADMINISTRATIVE INSTRUCTIONS ISSUED IN
CONJUNCTION WITH 52ND BATTALION MANCHESTER
REGIMENT NO.1. DATED 31. 8. 19.
----

1. All tentage, tent boards, stores taken over from 52nd Royal Sussex Regiment, Stores not brought by the Battalion from Geistingen, will be handed over.

2. As much stores as possible will be sent to Geistingen on Monday the 1st September. Companies etc. will form local dumps of Stores they cannot move on Transport allotted to them by Operation Order No.1. and notify the Q.M. of location.
Q.M. will move these dumps as transport becomes available.

3. Companies will revert to Company Messing as from Dinner 1st September. All Messing Equipment will be handed to "B" "D" and "HQ" Companies before 12.00 hours 1st September, and receipts obtained.
The Messing Officer will hand over to the Incoming Unit all requisitioned crockery.

4. All troops will be clear of Tents etc. by 09.00 hours on the 2nd September, weather permitting.
Tent flies will be rolled and tent Boards placed outside tents.

5. 1st Line Transport will be loaded by 18.00 hours 1st September "B" Company will supply loading party on application by Q.M.

[signature]

Lieut.
Act/Adjutant 52nd Battalion Manchester Regiment.

Copies to
1. War Diary.
2. "
3. C.O.
4. 2nd-in-Command.
5. "A" Company.
6. "B"   "
7. "C"   "
8. "D"   "
9. "HQ"   "
10. T.O.
11. Q.M.
12. R.S.M.
13. 3rd Bde. L.M.B.
14. O i/c Signals.
15. 3rd (Manchester) Infantry Bde.
16. 23rd Batt. Royal Fusiliers.
17. 51st King's Liverpool Regt.
18. 51st Batt. Manchester Regt.
19. File.

Army Form C. 2118.

WAR DIARY of the 52ND BN.
INTELLIGENCE SUMMARY. THE MANCHESTER REGT.
(Erase heading not required.)

Instructions regarding War Diaries and Intelligence Summaries are contained in F.S. Regs., Part II and the Staff Manual respectively. Title pages will be prepared in manuscript.

Sheet 1.

Place	Date	Hour	Summary of Events and Information	Remarks and references to Appendices
GEISTINGEN (1)	2.10.19	0900	Billeting of Batt. commenced. H.Q. Coy. heavy taken over all billets in "BONNER STR. GEISTINGEN. "B" Coy prepared to move into the CONVENT School and SKITTLE ALLEY, numerous huts having been requisitioned. "D" Coy all billets in ROTT.	Rutterfield ?
(2)	3.10.19	0830	CONVENT SCHOOL cleared out and beds installed ready for "B" Coy to move in at 1400 hrs. Much rain having fallen in last few days billets all tend to left standing.	
(3)	4.10.19		Training of horses and mules for jumping and polo at Brigade Horse Show commenced. All mules very obstinate.	
(4)	5.10.19		B Coy moved into billets at the convent school and the Garden city Geistingen. Training of animals continues. Retraining of mules with donkey stitches as a Much polo played on numerous whilst hockey football.	
(5)	6.10.19			
(6)	7.10.19		A Coy moved into Ebarty, Hall, Keuney, L.M.B. into Jacobi's factory Hennef.	
(7)	8.10.19		Brigade Horse Show held at HENNEF. Some excellent jumping seen. Polo on mules won by no. (Contd.)	

Army Form C. 2118.

WAR DIARY
or
INTELLIGENCE SUMMARY.
(Erase heading not required.)

Sheet 2

Instructions regarding War Diaries and Intelligence Summaries are contained in F.S. Regs., Part II. and the Staff Manual respectively. Title pages will be prepared in manuscript.

Place	Date	Hour	Summary of Events and Information	Remarks and references to Appendices
(continued)			Officers riding school putting now by LIEUT BM ALEXANDER.	Nasa
S. GEISTINGEN	14.10.19		4 men report reception camp from leave in UK, being the first return since the strikes are settled.	Report
"	16.10.19		Reception camp moved into billets a JACOBI's factory HENNEF. Ratm.	Report
"	19.10.19		Rugby match against X Corps Troops. BONN.	Support
"	20.10.19		Full scheme of reorganisation received. Arrangements made with 53 MANCHESTERS.	Support
"	21.10.19		Semi-final Polo on mules. Made wrestling & pillow fighting at pin transport field	Support
"	22.10.19		Conference of Commanding Officers at 52 Plans HQ. Re. Re-organisation.	Support
"	23.10.19		3rd Brigade Horse Show held at HENNEF	Support
"	24.10.19		Lt.-Col. W.J. Woodcock D.S.O. 13th Lancashire Fusiliers joined the Batt. prior to taking over command.	
"	24.10.19		Batt. absorbed 16 Officers 570 O.R's of 53rd Manchester Regt. under Rhine Army	
"	25.10.19		Reorganisation scheme.	
"	26.10.19		Day devoted to inspections and checking of stores, equipment etc.	
"	27.10.19		Lt-Col S.E. Kelly D.S.O. left the Batt. to take over command of the 20th K.R.R. Rev. H.A. William C.F. left the Batt. & proceeded to join the 51st Manc.	

WAR DIARY
or
INTELLIGENCE SUMMARY.

Army Form C. 2118.

Sheet 3

Place	Date	Hour	Summary of Events and Information	Remarks and references to Appendices
20	28/9/19		Demonstration Potted Athletic Meets by "A" Coy	
21	29/9/19		Major-Gen Solly-Flood visited the Batt. C.B. CMG DSO	
22	30/9/19		Batt. visited by Major-Gen. Hennaker commanding Scottish Division	
23	31/10/19		Batt visited by Major-Gen Solly-Flood C.B. CMG. D.S.O.	

W Wosnow
Lt. Colonel
Comdg 2/6 52nd Bn Manchester Regt.

ORDERLY ROOM.
3 7 OCT 1919
62nd Bn.
MANCHESTER REGT.